WHAT U LL GET

FROM THIS

"Parenting 3.0"

Book?

- Over 25,000 parents used this 12 Re -Parenting Tools.
- A proven DIY formula for the last 25 years.
- You can diagnose ur parenting style in 5 minutes.
- You can become no1 kid Psychologist for grooming ur Genius kids.
- Dr P T sunderam, Asia's Top1% Parenting 3.0 Mentor, teaches the same Model to "Parenting Coaches" the last 30 years.

drsuntrg@gmail.com

12 Re-Parenting Tools ©
Dr.PT.Sunderam

Zoo Parenting System

Made with ❤ on the Notion Press Platform
www.notionpress.com

Contents   Page No

How to Become a Parenting Psychologist for Your Kid
1. Go through the self-test and diagnose your own parenting style.
2. Fill in the form for your kids and email us.
3. Go through the YouTube video link for every parenting style. (Sorry not hyperlinked)
4. Similarly identify your kid's learning style.
5. Sketch your kid's genius grooming pattern.

Voice of our parenting clients

This is how my son suffered with Wrong career.....

Mr. Dillip

(4 years ago)

★★★★★

I recommend the doctor
Happy with: Doctor friendliness Explanation of the health issue Treatment Satisfaction Value for Money Wait time
Im a graduate working in BPO went to doctor for psychological issues. Doctor was very friendly.
Spoke over the phone first and asked to write email first about my issues did a pre diagnosis that I have personality disturbance. Had one session.
Happy with the outcome. I understood I've chosen wrong Career and I'm a creative person. Was told to do some home work and eager about the second session

Dr. P T Sunderam (PhD) replied
Client was very committed to improve, the way he did the home work before coming for counseling session was itself a proof of his seriousness, the best part of the session goes to his wife who silently was serving as bridge of communication between us Because of lack of appropriate career guidance know ledge from school r from specialist have made my client choose an accident at job which was not in tune to his Passion The client is coming for womb based career guidance test,which gives an indication of his passionate areas towards professional success

A 10   Mr. Dillip

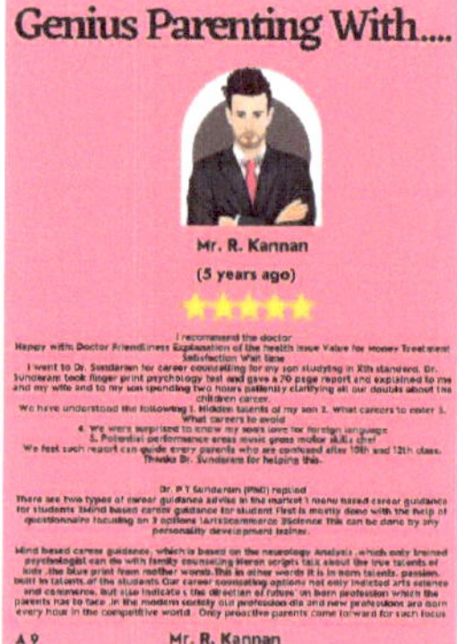

Genius Parenting With....

Mr. R. Kannan

(5 years ago)

★★★★★

I recommend the doctor
Happy with: Doctor Friendliness Explanation of the health issue Value for Money Treatment Satisfaction Wait time
I went to Dr. Sundaram for career counselling for my son studying in Xth standard. Dr. Sundaram took finger print psychology test and gave a 70 page report and explained to me and my wife and to my son spending two hours patiently clarifying all our doubts about the children career.
We have understood the following 1. Hidden talents of my son 2. What careers to enter 3. What careers to avoid
4. We were surprised to know my son's love for foreign language
5. Potential performance areas music gross motor skills chef
We feel such report can guide every parents who are confused after 10th and 12th class. Thanks Dr. Sundaram for helping this.

Dr. P T Sundaram (PhD) replied
There are two types of career guidance advise in the market 1 menu based career guidance for students 2kind based career guidance for student First is mostly done with the help of questionnaire focusing on 3 options 1Arts2commerce 3Science This can be done by any personality development trainer.

Mind based career guidance, which is based on the neurology Analysis ,which only trained psychologist can do with family counseling Heron scripts talk about the true talents of kids ,the blue print from mother womb.This in other words it is in born talents, passion, built in talents of the students Our career counselling options not only inclcted arts science and commerce, but also indicate s the direction of future' on born profession which the parents has to face ,in the modern society old profession die and new professions are born every hour in the competitive world . Only proactive parents come forward for such focus

A 9   Mr. R. Kannan

For further testimonials click below

https://www.practo.com/chennai/therapist/dr-p-t-sunderam

Dr.PT Sunderam

Dr PT Sunderam is India's First Neuro Parenting Mentor, an expert in re-programming the subconscious mind habits of the kids. Over the past 25 years, he has helped over 25000 young parents, teaching and training scientific parenting system. (How to diagnose their kid's problems with '12 Re-parenting tools' and help them groom as genius kids.). He is a post-graduate in Counselling & Psychotherapy, he also holds a PhD in neuro-linguistic psychology. Dr P.T. Sunder has applied NLP (subconscious mind therapy) successfully for a prisoner of Hyderabad Central jail in 2002 and got a Cash award of Rs 1 lakh.

Dr. PT Sunderam is trained under Dr. Richard Bandelr NLP founder and Dr. John Gray Mar, Venus Neuro Parenting Expert of the world. He conducts workshops for young parents on a wide range of issues. Dr. Sunderam has pioneered NLP movement in India; He is passionate about coaching and believes that healthy relationships can add meaning and fulfillment to our lives.

His mission is to empower 1 million young parents to lead legendary life for the next generation. Dr. PT Sunderam's work is in social media with over 1000+ YouTube videos and podcasts in 4 languages (English /Hindi/Telugu/Tamil).

Contact -drsuntrg@gmail.com

register.ptsneuroparenting.com.

BOOK HERE

FREE CONSULTANCY COUPONS

Kindly fill in the form with the eligibility criteria
and
enclose screenshot evidence to email

"drsuntrg@gmail.com"

Client Intake Form

Mother Name: ______________________________

Age of the mother: ______________________________

City : ______________________________

Phone Number: ______________________________

Email: ______________________________

Eligibility Criteria

(within the first 10 days of purchase of the book)

1. I have read the book ____________________ (mention the title of the book)

2. I am impressed with ____________________ (chapter of the book)

3. I am including the screenshot of the lines for clarification (screenshot)

    3.1 Name of the kid _______

    3.2 Age of the kid _______

    3.3 Mother tongue of the kid _______

    3.4 Residing city _______

4. I am including the photo of me and my kid

5. I want consultation for the following three points

(i) ____

____

(ii) ____

____

(iii) ____

____

Why you should read this book?
(A Parenting Self Diagnosis approach)

Are you tired of traditional parenting or Google parenting approaches that just don't seem to work? As a parenting coach with over 25 years of experience and 25,000 young parents under my guidance, I've developed a breakthrough approach to parenting - the "Animal style" of parenting. For the last 25 years, I've kept this diagnostic parenting approach a secret, using it to help mothers like you, master the skills of molding "Troublesome kids into Genius kids" in just 4 hours of training with my Genius Parenting Mastery skills. In this book, I'm finally sharing my secret approach with you.

The "Animal style" of parenting is based on breakthrough science and offers a fresh perspective on how to raise happy, healthy, and successful children. With my approach, you'll learn the brain factory with genius parenting training and how to tap into your child's natural instincts and behaviors, trying to suppress or control them. You'll discover how to communicate effectively, build trust and respect, and foster independence and creativity in your child.

And with my Genius Parenting Mastery skills training, you'll have access to a proven system that can transform even the most challenging parent-child relationships. So, if you're ready to become the best parent you can be and unlock your child's full potential, order your copy of my book today and take the first step towards a brighter future for your family.

As a parenting coach, I have helped countless young mothers overcome the challenges of raising "troublesome" kids and turn them into "genius" kids. My secret? Genius Parenting Training, a powerful four-hour program that teaches essential parenting skills.

I work with mothers one-on-one, offering personalized support and guidance based on their unique situation. Through this approach, I have helped mothers transform their children's behavior in just a few short hours. Here are three examples of mothers I've worked with who have seen incredible results: Sarah was struggling to manage her five-year-old's tantrums and aggressive behavior.

After just one session of Genius Parenting Training, she saw a dramatic improvement in her son's behavior and was able to handle tantrums with ease. Lisa was dealing with a rebellious teenager who was constantly pushing boundaries. Through our training, she learned how to communicate effectively with her daughter and set boundaries in a way that built trust and respect. Karen had a three-year-old who was struggling with socialization and communication skills. With my guidance, she was able to foster her child's creativity and independence, resulting in significant improvements in her social and communication abilities.

If you're a young mother struggling with parenting challenges, don't wait any longer to get the support you need. Contact me today to learn more about Genius Parenting Training and how it can help you transform your child's behavior in just four hours.

Acknowledgment

"I would like to express my gratitude to my editor, who has been a tireless advocate for this book and has provided invaluable guidance and support throughout the writing and editing process. Finally, I would like to thank the readers of this book, whose interest and support make all the hard work and long hours worthwhile. Thank you for joining me on this journey, and I hope that this book will provide you with insights, inspiration, and new perspectives."

– Dr.PT Sunderam

What is your parenting style ? (Self-Test)

Certainly! Below is a questionnaire designed to identify the 12 Re-parenting styles

Name of Kid ________________

Age of kid ______________

Name of the mother ________________

Contact no ______________ Email id ______________________

Instruction for filling up

1. There are 12 questions, styles and each question talks of a specific talent or demonstrated behaviour as an indicator in the development stages of the kids.
2. Each type has options; select a maximum, as observed in the kid's behaviour.
3. After filling up the response, find the maximum number of responses for each type. (Mark Y for yes and N for no)
4. The maximum (number of yes) against the style type becomes the domain style of the kid, and he rest becomes the secondary talent of the kid.
5. For expert advice, send to drsuntrg@gmail.com.

1. Honeybee style

How does your child typically react when faced with a new or unfamiliar situation?

a) They approach it with excitement and curiosity....................(Y/N)
b) They observe cautiously before deciding how to proceed....(Y/N)
c) They confidently take charge and try to lead others.............(Y/N)
d) They seek reassurance and guidance from trusted adults....Y/N)
e) They tend to withdraw or become anxious.............................Y/N)

2. Elephant style

When playing with others, which statement best describes your child's behaviour?

a) They enjoy being the centre of attention and engaging others in fun activities...Y/N)
b) They prefer one-on-one interactions or playing independently ....(Y/N)
c) They like to organise games and direct others to play..........(Y/N)
d) They are empathetic and often take on the role of mediator ....(Y/N)
e) They may be reserved or selective about who they play with ....(Y/N)

3. Cheetah style

How does your child handle criticism or correction from authority figures?

a) They take it in stride and use it as an opportunity for growth ....(Y/N)
b) They may become quiet or introspective, processing the feedback internally ....(Y/N)
c) They may resist or argue against criticism, defending their actions ....(Y/N)
d) They strive to please authority figures and may become overly compliant ....(Y/N)
e) They may internalise criticism and become overly self-critical..(Y/N)

4. Cat style

When facing a challenge or obstacle, what is your child's initial response?

a) They tackle it head-on with enthusiasm and determination......(Y/N)
b) They assess the situation and consider different approaches before acting ....(Y/N)

   c) They may try to find a quick solution or seek assistance from others..(Y/N)
   d) They may feel overwhelmed and seek support from trusted individuals ....(Y/N)
   e) They may avoid the challenge altogether or become indecisive ....(Y/N)

5. Owl style

How does your child typically express their emotions?

   a) They are expressive and may wear their emotions on their sleeve ....(Y/N)
   b) They may keep their emotions to themselves until they feel safe to share ....(Y/N)
   c) They express emotions openly and may be prone to dramatic displays ....(Y/N)
   d) They are sensitive to the emotions of others and may try to comfort them ....(Y/N)
   e) They may struggle to identify or express their emotions clearly ....(Y/N)

6. Puppy style

How does your child respond to rules or authority?

   a) They may challenge rules that seem arbitrary or restrictive ....(Y/N)
   b) They generally follow rules but may question them if they don't understand the reasoning ....(Y/N)
   c) They may try to bend or manipulate rules to suit their own agenda ....(Y/N)
   d) They strive to follow rules to maintain harmony and avoid conflict...(Y/N)
   e) They may feel stifled or rebellious in response to rules........(Y/N)

7. Dolphin style

In social situations, how does your child interact with others?

a) They enjoy being the life of the party and engaging everyone in conversation ....(Y/N)
b) They may be more reserved, observing others before joining in...(Y/N)
c) They may take charge and initiate activities or discussions .....(Y/N)
d) They are attentive listeners and may offer support to those in need..(Y/N)
e) They may feel uncomfortable in large social settings or prefer one-on-one interactions............................(Y/N)

8. Lion style

How does your child handle change or unpredictability?

a) They may embrace change and see it as an opportunity for adventure ....(Y/N)
b) They may feel uneasy but adapt quickly once they understand the new situation ....(Y/N)
c) They may resist change and prefer the comfort of familiar routines...(Y/N)
d) They may seek reassurance and guidance from trusted individuals ....(Y/N)
e) They may become anxious or overwhelmed by change ....(Y/N)

9. Dove style

What motivates your child the most?

a) They are driven by a desire for new experiences and excitement..(Y/N)
b) They are motivated by a need for security and stability ....(Y/N)
c) They thrive on challenges and enjoy achieving goals or milestones ....(Y/N)

d) They are motivated by a desire to connect with others
and foster harmony ....(Y/N)
e) They may struggle to identify specific motivations or
may be motivated by avoiding negative outcomes ....(Y/N)

10. Peacock Style

When studying, which method helps your child understand information best?

a) Using colourful diagrams or charts...(Y/N)
b) Reading written instructions or text..(Y/N)
c) Watching educational videos or presentations ....(Y/N)
d) Observing demonstrations or examples ....(Y/N)
e) Using flashcards or visual aids..(Y/N)

11. Fox Style

How does your child prefer to learn new concepts or vocabulary?

a) Listening to recorded lectures or podcasts ....(Y/N)
b) Participating in group discussions or study sessions ....(Y/N)
c) Reading aloud to yourself or someone else..........................(Y/N)
d) Using mnemonic devices or rhymes to remember
information..(Y/N)
e) Explaining concepts to others verbally ....(Y/N)

12. Bonobo Style

When learning a new skill, what approach does your child find most effective?

a) Practicing the skill repeatedly until mastered ....(Y/N)
b) Using physical objects or manipulatives to
understand concepts...(Y/N)
c) Engaging in hands-on activities or experiments...................(Y/N)
d) Moving around or pacing while studying ....(Y/N)
e) Taking breaks to engage in physical activity before
returning to study ....(Y/N)

Answers

(Key to your score, select the maximum score as primary behavior,)
(type or style is used to denote the same behavior)

1. TYPE 1 - The Honeybee: These children are often responsible, rule-abiding, and strive for excellence. They may be conscientious and detail-oriented, with a strong sense of right and wrong.

2. TYPE 2 - The Elephant: These children are caring, nurturing, and empathetic. They often seek to please others and may go out of their way to be helpful and supportive.

3. TYPE 3 - The Cheetah: These children are ambitious, driven, and goal-oriented. They thrive on success and may be competitive, seeking recognition and approval from others.

4. TYPE 4 - The Cat: These children are creative, introspective, and sensitive. They may have a rich inner world and express themselves through art, music, or storytelling.

5. TYPE 5 - The Dolphin: These children are curious, analytical, and independent thinkers. They enjoy learning and may prefer solitary activities that allow them to explore their interests deeply.

6. TYPE 6 - The Puppy: These children are loyal, cautious, and security-oriented. They may seek reassurance from trusted adults and may be diligent about following rules and routines.

7. TYPE 7 - The Dolphin: These children are energetic, adventurous, and optimistic. They enjoy new experiences and may have a playful, spontaneous approach to life.

8. TYPE 8 - The Lion: These children are assertive, confident, and independent. They may be natural leaders who aren't afraid to speak their minds and stand up for themselves and others.

9. TYPE 9 - The Dove: These children are easygoing, agreeable, and harmonious. They may seek to avoid conflict and may go along with others' preferences to maintain peace and stability.

10. TYPE 10 - Peacock style: Children who prefer visual learning tend to excel with images, diagrams, and written instructions. They may benefit from using visual aids during study sessions and prefer to process information by seeing it.

11. TYPE 11 - Fox style: Children who prefer auditory learning thrive on verbal explanations, discussions, and listening to lectures or audiobooks. They may prefer to study in environments where they can listen to verbal instructions or music.

12. TYPE 12 - Bonobo: Children who prefer kinesthetic learning learn best through hands-on activities, physical demonstrations, and movement. They may enjoy interactive learning experiences and benefit from engaging in activities that involve physical manipulation

Chapter 1: Honey Bee Parenting Style

Parents who embrace the Honey Bee Parenting Style prioritize structure and organization in their children's life. They establish routines and schedules that provide a sense of stability and predictability. By setting clear expectations and boundaries, they help their children develop a strong sense of responsibility and self-discipline. These parents value punctuality, cleanliness, and orderliness, instilling these principles in their children's daily lives.

The Honey Bee Parenting Style emphasizes the importance of moral values and ethics. Parents lead by example, demonstrating honesty, integrity, and respect in their own actions and interactions. They teach their children the value of empathy, compassion, and fairness, encouraging them to treat others with kindness and understanding. These parents foster a strong moral compass in their children, helping them make ethical choices and develop a sense of social responsibility.

Furthermore, the Honey Bee Parenting Style nurtures character development. Parents encourage their children to take on responsibilities and contribute to the family or community. They support their children's efforts to pursue personal interests and hobbies, fostering a sense of purpose and passion. These parents also prioritize education, valuing knowledge acquisition, and encouraging their child's intellectual development.

By adopting the Honey Bee Parenting Style, parents create an environment that promotes structure, responsibility, and moral values. Children raised with this style develop self-discipline, a strong moral compass, and a sense of purpose. They grow up with a solid foundation for personal growth and character development, equipped to navigate life's challenges with integrity and resilience.

However, it is important for parents practicing the Honey Bee Parenting Style to balance structure and responsibility with flexibility and adaptability. They should also allow room for their children's individuality and creativity to nourish. By striking this balance, parents can cultivate an environment that combines structure and moral values with the freedom for their children to explore their unique interests and passions, leading to holistic growth and character development.

Example 1:

Good Honey Bee Parenting Style (Indian name: Anika)

Anika exemplifies the positive aspects of the Honey Bee Parenting Style. She provides a structured and responsible environment for her child's growth and character development. Anika establishes consistent routines and schedules that promote stability and organization. She teaches her child the importance of punctuality, cleanliness, and orderliness.

Anika leads by example, displaying honesty, integrity, and respect in her own actions and interactions. She instills moral values such as empathy, compassion, and fairness in her child, encouraging them to treat others with kindness and understanding. Anika supports her child's academic pursuits and extracurricular activities, valuing their intellectual development and fostering a sense of purpose. By embracing the Honey Bee Parenting Style, Anika creates a nurturing environment that cultivates responsibility, moral values, and personal growth in her child.

Example 2:

Bad Honey Bee Parenting Style (Indian name: Rohit)

Rohit represents a negative example of the Honey Bee Parenting Style. He takes the structured and responsible aspect to an extreme, becoming overly controlling and rigid. Rohit imposes strict routines and schedules on his child, leaving little room for flexibility or spontaneity. He becomes excessively focused on rules and orderliness, neglecting the importance of emotional connection and creativity. Rohit's approach lacks warmth and understanding, failing to prioritize empathy and compassion. He enforces moral values without explaining their significance, leading to a lack of genuine understanding and internalization in his child. Rohit's rigid style limits his child's individuality and interests, hindering their personal growth and character development. In this example, the Honey Bee Parenting Style is misapplied, resulting in a sitting and overly controlling environment.

https://www.youtube.com/watch?v=PCCm-B-kx6s

How a Mother can rewire
the Brain Factory
of your kids ?

" I help young parents
to mould
" War kids to Genius kids"
in 4 hours with
Genius Parenting Training "
-Dr.PT Sunderam

Contact
drsuntrg@gmail.com

Chapter 2: Elephant Parenting Style

Parents who embrace the Elephant Parenting Style exhibit traits such as attentiveness, patience, and a genuine concern for their children's well-being. They provide a structured routine and consistent boundaries, allowing children to feel safe and secure. These parents prioritize responsibility, teaching their children the importance of accountability and moral values. By setting clear expectations and providing guidance, they enable children to develop a sense of purpose and direction.

Moreover, the Elephant Parenting Style emphasizes empathy and emotional support. Parents encourage open communication, actively listening to their children's thoughts and feelings without judgment. This approach helps children develop healthy emotional intelligence and a strong sense of self-worth.

They learn to navigate and understand their own emotions and are more likely to exhibit empathy towards others.

In addition, the Elephant Parenting Style promotes unconditional love. Parents provide unwavering support and acceptance, regardless of their children's successes or failures. This creates a nurturing environment where children feel valued and loved for who they are, fostering a positive self-image and a healthy sense of self-esteem.

Overall, the Elephant Parenting Style offers a balanced and holistic approach to raising children. It prioritizes structure, responsibility, morality, empathy, and unconditional love. By adopting this style, parents can create an environment that facilitates their children's growth, character development, and emotional well-being.

Example 1:

Good Elephant Parenting Style (Indian name: Radha)

The Elephant Parenting Style, characterized by its structured, responsible, and moral approach, is an ideal method for nurturing your child's growth and character development. This style emphasizes creating a secure and supportive environment while instilling values of empathy and unconditional love.

Radha, a mother who embodies the principles of the Elephant Parenting Style, fosters her child's growth in a nurturing and structured manner. She encourages open communication, actively listens to her child's concerns, and provides a safe space for expression. Radha sets clear boundaries and teaches her child the importance of responsibility and moral values. She supports her child's interests, encouraging them to explore their passions while gently guiding them towards making informed decisions. Radha's love is unconditional, and she provides a warm, accepting environment where her child feels secure and valued. Through her consistent presence and empathetic approach, Radha nurtures her child's self-esteem and helps them develop a strong sense of character.

https://www.youtube.com/watch?v=meQWZ70uvo8

Example 2:

Bad Elephant Parenting Style (Indian name: Ramesh)

Ramesh represents a negative example of the Elephant Parenting Style. He is overprotective and excessively involved in his child's life. Ramesh shields his child from any potential hardships or challenges, hindering their personal growth. He hampers their autonomy by making decisions on their behalf, without considering their opinions or desires. Ramesh's love is conditional, and he often uses guilt or manipulation to control his child's behavior. As a result, the child becomes dependent and lacks a sense of personal agency. Ramesh's overbearing nature sties the child's individuality, and they struggle to develop their own moral compass and decision-making skills.

These examples highlight the stark contrast between good and bad Elephant Parenting Styles. The good style, embodied by Radha, cultivates a secure and supportive environment where children can thrive and develop character. On the other hand, the bad style, represented by Ramesh, inhibits a child's growth, independence, and self-esteem. By adopting the positive aspects of the Elephant Parenting Style, parents can effectively nurture their children, fostering their emotional well-being and character development.)

Chapter 3: Cheetah Parenting Style

Parents who adopt the Cheetah Parenting Style instill in their children a strong drive to succeed. They encourage goal-setting and teach the value of hard work, determination, and perseverance. These parents believe in the potential of their children and provide the necessary support and resources to help them excel in their chosen pursuits. They inspire their children to dream big and instill in them the belief that they can achieve their goals with dedication and effort.

The Cheetah Parenting Style emphasizes the importance of maintaining a healthy balance in life. While encouraging their children to strive for success, these parents also recognize the significance of other aspects, such as relationships, personal well-being, and enjoyment. They teach their children the importance of self-care, time management, and setting boundaries to prevent burnout and maintain a harmonious life.

By adopting the positive aspects of the Cheetah Parenting Style, parents empower their children to pursue their dreams while maintaining a balanced and fulfilling life. They cultivate resilience and a growth mindset, teaching their children to view failures as opportunities for learning and growth. These children grow up with a strong work ethic, the ability to set and achieve goals, and the skills necessary to navigate challenges and setbacks.

The Cheetah Parenting Style, when practiced effectively, promotes self-confidence, ambition, and a drive for success, to equip children with valuable skills and attitudes that can benefit them throughout their lives. However, it is important for parents to strike a balance, ensuring that the pursuit of success does not overshadow the well-being and overall development of their children.

Example 1:

Good Cheetah Parenting Style (Indian name: Aarav):

Aarav, a parent who embraces the positive aspects of the Cheetah Parenting Style, encourages his child to set ambitious goals and supports them throughout their journey. He provides guidance and resources to help his child excel in their chosen pursuits. Aarav fosters a growth mindset in his child, emphasizing that failure is a stepping stone to success. He celebrates his child's achievements and teaches them the value of hard work and perseverance. However, Aarav also ensures that his child maintains a balance in life, encouraging them to engage in activities that promote their overall well-being, such as spending time with family and pursuing hobbies.

Example 2:

Bad Cheetah Parenting Style (Indian name: Neha):

Neha represents a negative example of the Cheetah Parenting Style. She places an overwhelming emphasis on success and achievement, pushing her child to constantly outperform others. Neha's parenting revolves solely around external validation and accolades. She sets unrealistic expectations and exerts excessive pressure on her child, often neglecting their emotional well-being. This constant drive for success leaves the child feeling burnt out, stressed, and disconnected from their own desires and passions. The child may develop a fear of failure and may struggle to find their true sense of identity and purpose.

Good Cheetah parenting empowers children to pursue their dreams while maintaining a healthy work-life balance and emphasizing personal growth and well-being. In contrast, bad Cheetah parenting can lead to undue stress, anxiety, and a lack of fulfillment in a child's life. By adopting the positive aspects of the Cheetah Parenting Style and avoiding its pitfalls, parents can guide their children towards success while prioritizing their holistic development and overall happiness.

https://www.youtube.com/watch?v=J2dEHu1aSWI

How a Mother can rewire
the Brain Factory
of your kids ?

" I help young parents
to mould
" War kids to Genius kids"
in 4 hours with
Genius Parenting Training "
-Dr.PT Sunderam

Contact
drsuntrg@gmail.com

Chapter 4: Cat Parenting Style

The Cat Parenting Style encourages an environment that nurtures a child's imagination and creativity. Parents who adopt this style provide opportunities for their children to engage in artistic and expressive activities, such as drawing, painting, writing, or playing musical instruments. They support their children's exploration of different forms of self-expression, allowing them to discover and develop their own creative talents and interests.

Moreover, the Cat Parenting Style values emotional depth and authenticity. Parents prioritize open communication and encourage their children to express their emotions freely. They create a safe space where children feel comfortable discussing their feelings, fears, and aspirations. By validating their emotions, parents help their children develop healthy emotional intelligence and a strong sense of self.

The Cat Parenting Style also emphasizes embracing a child's unique identity and individuality. Parents encourage their children to explore their interests and passions, even if they deviate from societal norms or expectations. They celebrate their children's quirks, talents, and differences, fostering a sense of self-acceptance and self-confidence.

By embracing the Cat Parenting Style, parents enable their children to develop a rich inner world, a deep appreciation for art and creativity, and a strong sense of self-identity. Children raised with this style are likely to be introspective, imaginative, and empathetic towards others.

It is important for parents practicing the Cat Parenting Style to balance their children's creative and emotional needs with practical life skills and external experiences. While encouraging self-expression, they should also ensure that their children have the necessary skills to navigate the realities of the world. By nurturing their children's creativity and emotional depth within a supportive and balanced framework, parents can help them cultivate a lifelong appreciation for art, individuality, and self-expression.

Example 1:

Good Cat Parenting Style (Indian name: Anaya)

Anaya, a parent who embodies the positive aspects of the Cat Parenting Style, encourages her child's creativity and emotional depth. She provides a nurturing environment where her child can explore various artistic forms and express themselves freely. Anaya supports her child's interests in painting and writing, providing the necessary materials and opportunities for creative expression.

She engages in open and honest conversations with her child, allowing them to freely share their emotions and thoughts. Anaya celebrates her child's uniqueness and encourages them to embrace their individuality, fostering a sense of self-acceptance and confidence. She encourages her child to attend art classes and workshops, connecting them with a community of like-minded individuals. Through her supportive and accepting approach, Anaya nurtures her child's creative talents and emotional well-being.

Example 2:

Bad Cat Parenting Style (Indian name: Rahul)

Rahul represents a negative example of the Cat Parenting Style. He disregards his child's creative and emotional needs, emphasizing practicality and societal norms instead. Rahul discourages his child from pursuing artistic interests, believing that they will not lead to a stable career. He dismisses or belittles their creative endeavours, undermining their self-confidence and stumbling their creativity. Rahul dismisses or suppresses discussions about emotions, deeming them unnecessary or weak. As a result, his child struggles with emotional expression and may feel disconnected from their own feelings. The child may develop a sense of self-doubt and may struggle with self-acceptance due to the lack of support

E book free

Reverse 3 mistakes of
Parenting with 12
parenting tools
1 scrren time 2 shykid
3 shouting and yelling

switch from

Google parentings skills

to

scientifc parenting skills

from their parent. Rahul's restrictive approach limits his child's potential for self-expression and hampers their emotional well-being.

These examples highlight the contrast between good and bad Cat Parenting Styles. The good style, represented by Anaya, nurtures a child's creativity, emotional depth, and individuality, fostering their overall well-being. On the other hand, the bad style, exemplified by Rahul, neglects or suppresses a child's creative and emotional needs, hindering their self-expression and personal growth. By adopting the positive aspects of the Cat Parenting Style, parents can empower their children to embrace their uniqueness and foster their creativity and emotional well-being.

https://www.youtube.com/watch?v=_6vbL9Nl3B4

Chapter 5: Owl Parenting Style

Parents who adopt the Owl Parenting Style prioritize intellectual growth and create an environment that values knowledge. They provide ample opportunities for their children to explore various subjects and encourage independent thinking. These parents stimulate their children's intellectual curiosity by engaging in meaningful conversations, asking thought-provoking questions, and exposing them to a wide range of educational resources.

The Owl Parenting Style promotes independence and self-reliance. Parents encourage their children to take responsibility for their own learning and decision-making processes. They empower their children to seek answers to their questions, conduct research, and develop problem-solving skills. By fostering independence, parents instill confidence and a sense of autonomy in their children, enabling them to become self-directed learners.

Furthermore, the Owl Parenting Style cultivates a love for knowledge. Parents encourage their children to explore various fields of interest, whether it be through books, documentaries, or hands-on experiences. They create a supportive environment where their children feel safe to experiment, make mistakes, and grow intellectually. These parents also act as role models, demonstrating their own passion for learning and engaging in intellectual pursuits.

By embracing the Owl Parenting Style, parents can nurture their children's natural curiosity and foster a love for lifelong learning. Children raised with this style are likely to develop critical thinking skills, a thirst for knowledge, and a sense of intellectual independence. They grow up with a deep appreciation for learning and are motivated to explore and understand the world around them.

It is important for parents practicing the Owl Parenting Style to balance intellectual stimulation with other aspects of their children's development. While encouraging intellectual growth, they should also prioritize their children's emotional well-being, social interactions, and physical activities. By creating a holistic approach to parenting, parents can cultivate a well-rounded individual who possesses both intellectual curiosity and a balanced lifestyle.

Example 1:

Good Owl Parenting Style (Indian name: Aarushi)

Aarushi embodies the positive aspects of the Owl Parenting Style. She creates an intellectually stimulating environment for her child, encouraging their curiosity and love for knowledge. Aarushi regularly engages in meaningful conversations with her child, exploring various topics and encouraging them to think critically. She provides a wide range of educational resources, such as books, educational games, and interactive learning platforms, to fuel her child's thirst for knowledge.

Aarushi supports her child's independent learning by allowing them to choose topics of interest and providing guidance as needed. She also fosters a love for learning by exposing her child to different cultural experiences, museums, and educational outings. Aarushi's nurturing approach to intellectual growth ensures her child develops a lifelong passion for learning and a strong foundation for future academic success.

Example 2:

Bad Owl Parenting Style (Indian name: Rohit)

Rohit represents a negative example of the Owl Parenting Style. He places excessive pressure on his child's intellectual abilities and neglects other aspects of their development. Rohit sets unrealistic expectations for academic achievement, constantly pushing his child to excel academically. He fails to provide a supportive environment for learning and exploration, emphasizing rote memorization over critical thinking. Rohit discourages independent thought and discourages his child from pursuing areas of interest outside the traditional academic curriculum. As a result, his child may develop a fear of failure, lack creativity, and may struggle with self-esteem issues. Rohit's approach to parenting limits his child's intellectual growth and hampers their overall development.

These examples highlight the importance of nurturing intellectual curiosity while maintaining a balanced approach to parenting. Good Owl parenting, like Aarushi's approach, fosters a love for knowledge and independent thinking. On the other hand, bad Owl parenting, as demonstrated by Rohit, sties intellectual growth and neglects the holistic development of the child. By embracing the positive aspects of the Owl Parenting Style, parents can create an intellectually stimulating environment that encourages curiosity, critical thinking, and a lifelong love for learning in their children.

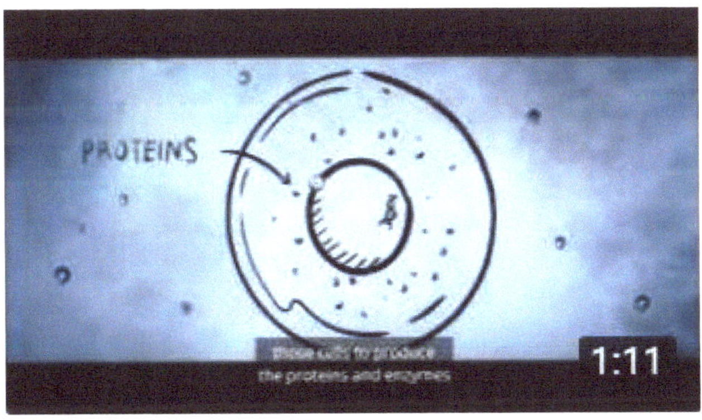

https://www.youtube.com/watch?v=mLu5uXwGlww

How a Mother can rewire
the Brain Factory
of your kids ?

" I help young parents
to mould
" War kids to Genius kids"
in 4 hours with
Genius Parenting Training "
-Dr.PT Sunderam

Contact
drsuntrg@gmail.com

Chapter 6: The Puppy Parenting Style

Parents who adopt the Puppy Parenting Style prioritize creating a secure and loving environment for their children. They establish clear boundaries and consistent routines, offering a sense of stability and predictability. These parents provide guidance and support, acting as a reliable source of comfort and reassurance. They prioritize open communication and actively listen to their children's concerns and fears, providing guidance and empathy to address their emotional needs.

The Puppy Parenting Style emphasizes the importance of trust and loyalty. Parents build a foundation of trust with their children by being reliable and dependable. They fulfill promises and commitments, demonstrating their loyalty and establishing a strong bond with their child. These parents foster a sense of security and belonging, allowing their children to develop a positive self-image and build healthy relationships with others.

Moreover, parents practicing the Puppy Parenting Style instill a sense of responsibility and preparedness in their children. They teach them practical life skills, such as problem-solving, decision-making, and self-care, empowering them to navigate challenges with confidence. These parents encourage their children to develop a support network and seek help when needed, emphasizing the importance of interdependence and community.

By embracing the Puppy Parenting Style, parents create a nurturing and secure environment where children can thrive. Children raised with this style feel safe, loved, and supported, which positively impacts their emotional well-being and overall development. They grow up with a strong foundation of trust, resilience, and a sense of belonging.

It is important for parents practicing the Puppy Parenting Style to balance their desire to protect and reassure their children with allowing them to develop independence and resilience. By providing guidance and support while also fostering their children's autonomy, parents can help their children navigate the world with confidence and develop healthy coping mechanisms.

Example 1:

Good Puppy Parenting Style (Indian name: Aarav)

Aarav embodies the positive aspects of the Puppy Parenting Style. He creates a secure and trusting environment for his child, providing guidance and reassurance. Aarav establishes consistent routines and clear boundaries, which helps his child feel safe and know what to expect. He actively listens to his child's concerns and fears, offering support and understanding. Aarav builds a strong foundation of trust with his child by consistently following through on his commitments and being dependable. He encourages his child to take on age-appropriate responsibilities, teaching them practical life skills and fostering their independence. Aarav's nurturing approach allows his child to develop a sense of security, resilience, and a strong bond with their family.

Example 2:

Bad Puppy Parenting Style (Indian name: Meera)

Meera represents a negative example of the Puppy Parenting Style. She fails to provide a secure and loyal environment for her child, lacking guidance and reassurance. Meera neglects consistent routines and boundaries, which leaves her child feeling uncertain and anxious. She dismisses or ignores her child's concerns, failing to address their emotional needs.

Meera struggles with reliability and often breaks promises, leading to a lack of trust and a strained relationship with her child. She hinders her child's independence by being overprotective and not allowing them to take on age-appropriate responsibilities. Meera's parenting style creates insecurity and a lack of confidence in her child, impeding their emotional well-being and overall development.

These examples highlight the importance of providing a secure and trusting environment for children. Good Puppy parenting, like Aarav's approach, fosters a sense of stability, trust, and guidance. In contrast, bad Puppy parenting, as demonstrated by Meera, neglects the emotional needs of the child and lacks consistency, leading to insecurity and strained relationships. By embracing the positive aspects of the Puppy Parenting Style, parents can create a nurturing and loving environment that supports their children's need for guidance and reassurance.

https://www.youtube.com/watch?v=dusGp64oISs

Chapter 7: The Dolphin Parenting Style

Dolphin parents understand the importance of fostering a positive and lively environment for their children. They encourage exploration and provide ample opportunities for their children's imagination to nourish. These parents recognize the value of playfulness and encourage their children to engage in activities that ignite their passion and bring them joy. By embracing their children's sense of adventure, Dolphin parents create an environment that stimulates their curiosity and allows them to discover new interests and talents.

However, Dolphin parents also understand the need for balance. They recognize that while exploration and excitement are essential, structure and discipline are equally important for their children's development. They provide guidance to help their children learn to prioritize their activities and manage their time effectively. By instilling a sense of focus, Dolphin parents teach their children how to balance their adventurous spirit with responsibilities and commitments.

Dolphin parents are supportive and actively engage with their children, fostering open communication and a strong emotional connection. They listen attentively to their child's ideas and encourage them to express themselves freely. By providing a safe and nurturing space, Dolphin parents help their children develop self-confidence and self-expression.

In this chapter, we explored practical strategies and techniques for Dolphin parenting. We discussed how to encourage creativity, embrace spontaneity, and instill a sense of focus and balance in your child's life. By adopting the Dolphin Parenting Style, you can cultivate an environment that allows your child to embrace their curiosity, find joy in their pursuits, and develop into well-rounded individuals with a zest for life.

Example 1:

Good Dolphin Parenting Style (Indian name: Maya)

Maya embodies the positive aspects of the Dolphin Parenting Style. She creates a nurturing and supportive environment for her child's growth and development. Maya values open communication and active listening, fostering a strong emotional connection with her child. She encourages her child's curiosity and creativity, providing opportunities for exploration and self-expression. Maya promotes a balance between structure and flexibility, allowing her child to experience a sense of freedom while also providing clear boundaries. She prioritizes emotional well-being and teaches her child skills such as empathy, compassion, and conflict resolution. Maya nurtures her child's self-esteem and encourages a healthy balance between independence and interdependence. By embracing the Dolphin Parenting Style, Maya helps her child develop resilience, social skills, and a positive self-image.

Example 2:

Bad Dolphin Parenting Style (Indian name: Rajat)

Rajat represents a negative example of the Dolphin Parenting Style. He lacks emotional atonement and fails to prioritize his child's well-being. Rajat is distant and uninvolved in his child's life, lacking open communication and emotional connection. He imposes rigid rules and expectations without considering his child's individuality and needs. Rajat's parenting style is characterized by harsh criticism and a focus on achievement, neglecting the importance of nurturing his child's emotional development. He lacks empathy and fails to provide a supportive environment. Rajat's approach inhibits his child's self-expression, creativity, and emotional well-being. In this example, the Dolphin Parenting Style is misapplied, resulting in an environment that sties growth, emotional connection, and personal fulfillment.

These examples highlight the importance of adopting the Dolphin Parenting Style in a positive and balanced manner. Good dolphin parenting, like Maya's approach, promotes emotional connection, communication, and creativity while providing a nurturing and supportive environment. On the other hand, bad dolphin parenting, as demonstrated by Rajat, lacks emotional attunement, imposes rigid rules, and neglects the importance of emotional well-being and individuality. By prioritizing emotional connection, nurturing creativity, and fostering a supportive environment, parents can embrace the Dolphin Parenting Style to help their children thrive emotionally, socially, and intellectually.

https://www.youtube.com/watch?v=DSt93Mrz45Q

How a Mother can rewire
the Brain Factory
of your kids ?

" I help young parents
to mould
" War kids to Genius kids"
in 4 hours with
Genius Parenting Training "
-Dr.PT Sunderam

Contact
drsuntrg@gmail.com

Chapter 8: The Lion Parenting Style

Parents who adopt the Lion Parenting Style demonstrate strong leadership qualities. They establish clear and consistent boundaries, ensuring their children understand the expectations and consequences of their actions. These parents exhibit confidence and assertiveness while providing guidance and discipline. They are role models for their children, displaying integrity, accountability, and a strong sense of justice.

The Lion Parenting Style emphasizes respect in parent-child interactions. Parents respect their child's individuality, opinions, and emotions. They encourage open and honest communication, creating an environment where their child feels comfortable expressing themselves. These parents actively listen to their child's perspectives and encourage them to voice their thoughts and feelings. They teach their child to respect others as well, promoting empathy, kindness, and inclusivity.

Furthermore, parents practicing the Lion Parenting Style provide opportunities for their child's personal growth and development. They encourage independence and self-reliance, allowing their child to make age-appropriate decisions and learn from their experiences. These parents support their children's ambitions and passions, providing resources and guidance to help them achieve their goals. They foster a sense of resilience, teaching their children to overcome challenges and persevere in the face of adversity.

By embracing the Lion Parenting Style, parents can guide their children with strength, leadership, and assertiveness. children raised with this style learn to navigate the world confidently and responsibly. They develop a strong sense of self, respect for others, and the ability to assert their needs and boundaries. They grow up with a foundation of resilience and leadership skills, preparing them for success in various aspects of life.

However, it is essential for parents practicing the Lion Parenting Style to balance their assertiveness with empathy and flexibility. While setting firm boundaries, they should also create an environment that allows their children to express themselves and make choices within appropriate limits. By striking a balance between strength and compassion, parents can guide their children towards personal growth, self-confidence, and fulfilling their potential.

Example 1:

Good Lion Parenting Style (Indian name: Vikram)

Vikram embodies the positive aspects of the Lion Parenting Style. He demonstrates strong leadership and provides yet fair boundaries for his child. Vikram sets clear expectations and consequences, ensuring his child understands the importance of responsibility and accountability. He models integrity and treats his child with respect, valuing their opinions and emotions.

Vikram encourages open communication, actively listening to his child and involving them in decision-making processes. He provides opportunities for personal growth, supporting his child's interests and passions.

Vikram's nurturing approach instills confidence resilience, and a strong sense of leadership in his child.

Example 2:

Bad Lion Parenting Style (Indian name: Reena)

Reena represents a negative example of the Lion Parenting Style. She exhibits overly aggressive and authoritarian behavior, lacking respect and empathy towards her child. Reena sets strict and unreasonable boundaries, stressing her child's individuality and independence. She uses fear and intimidation as disciplinary methods, leading to a strained relationship and a lack of trust. Reena dismisses her child's opinions and emotions, failing to create a nurturing and supportive environment. She does not provide opportunities for personal growth and sties her child's ambitions and passions. Reena's parenting style hampers her child's self-esteem, confidence, and overall well-being.

These examples highlight the importance of balancing strength and leadership with respect, empathy, and flexibility. Good Lion parenting, like Vikram's approach, guides children with firm boundaries, respect, and opportunities for personal growth. In contrast, bad Lion parenting, as demonstrated by Reena, can be overly aggressive, lacking empathy, and hindering a child's development. By embracing the positive aspects of the Lion Parenting Style, parents can guide their children with strength, leadership, and assertiveness, while also nurturing their emotional well-being and supporting their individuality.

https://www.youtube.com/watch?v=DP3IjUZpfzU

Chapter 9: Dove Parenting Style

Parents who adopt the Dove Parenting Style prioritize creating a peaceful and inclusive environment for their children. They emphasize open and honest communication, encouraging their children to express their thoughts and emotions freely. These parents actively listen and validate their children's feelings, creating a safe space where their children feel heard and understood. They promote cooperation and collaboration, resolving conflicts through dialogue and compromise.

The Dove Parenting Style emphasizes creating a sense of belonging and harmony within the family.

Parents cultivate an atmosphere of acceptance and respect, valuing each family member's unique qualities and contributions. They promote inclusivity, celebrating diversity and encouraging their children to appreciate different perspectives and cultures. These parents prioritize building strong relationships and fostering a sense of unity and connection among family members.

Furthermore, parents practicing the Dove Parenting Style encourage their children's autonomy and decision-making skills. They provide opportunities for their children to express their preferences and make choices within appropriate limits. These parents value their children's individuality and support their personal interests and passions. They promote a peaceful and non-judgmental environment where their children can explore and develop their own identity.

By embracing the Dove Parenting Style, parents can foster open communication, understanding, and a sense of belonging for their children. Children raised with this style develop strong emotional intelligence, empathy, and conflict-resolution skills. They feel valued, supported, and connected within their family, leading to enhanced self-esteem and positive relationships with others.

However, it is important for parents practicing the Dove Parenting Style to maintain a balance between harmony and assertiveness. While prioritizing peace and understanding, they should also set appropriate boundaries and guide their child's behavior when necessary. By promoting open communication, acceptance, and a sense of belonging, parents can create a nurturing and harmonious environment where their children thrive emotionally and socially.

Example 1:

Good Dove Parenting Style (Indian name: Nisha)

Nisha embodies the positive aspects of the Dove Parenting Style. She creates a peaceful and harmonious environment for her child, fostering open communication and understanding.

Nisha encourages her child to express their thoughts and emotions, actively listening and validating their feelings. She promotes cooperation and collaboration, teaching her child the importance of resolving conflicts through dialogue and compromise. Nisha emphasizes acceptance and respect within the family, celebrating each family member's uniqueness and fostering a sense of belonging. She supports her child's autonomy, allowing them to make age-appropriate decisions and supporting their personal interests and passions. Nisha's nurturing approach cultivates emotional intelligence, empathy, and a strong sense of unity among family members.

Example 2:

Bad Dove Parenting Style (Indian name: Rahul)

Rahul represents a negative example of the Dove Parenting Style. He fails to create a peaceful and inclusive environment for his child, lacking open communication and understanding.

Rahul dismisses or ignores his child's thoughts and emotions, hindering their ability to express themselves. He avoids conflict rather than addressing it, leading to unresolved issues and a lack of emotional connection. Rahul neglects acceptance and respect within the family, failing to appreciate each family member's unique qualities. He sties his child's autonomy and individuality, imposing his own preferences and disregarding their interests and passions. Rahul's parenting style hampers his child's emotional well-being, self-expression, and sense of belonging within the family.

These examples highlight the importance of fostering open communication, understanding, and a sense of belonging within the family. Good Dove parenting, like Nisha's approach, creates a peaceful and inclusive environment where children feel heard, valued, and connected.

In contrast, bad Dove parenting, as demonstrated by Rahul, lacks open communication, understanding, and acceptance, hindering a child's emotional well-being and individuality. By embracing the positive aspects of the Dove Parenting Style, parents can nurture a harmonious and supportive environment where their child thrives emotionally and develops positive relationships.

https://www.youtube.com/watch?v=HF8BWQNV-ik

How a Mother can rewire
the Brain Factory
of your kids ?

" I help young parents
to mould
" War kids to Genius kids"
in 4 hours with
Genius Parenting Training "
-Dr.PT Sunderam

Contact
drsuntrg@gmail.com

Chapter 10: Peacock Parenting Style

Parents who adopt the Peacock Parenting Style recognize and celebrate their child's distinct qualities and talents. They create an environment that encourages self-expression and embraces their child's individuality. These parents provide opportunities for their child to explore their interests, hobbies, and creative pursuits. They value and nurture their child's unique strengths, allowing them to shine in their own way.

The Peacock Parenting Style emphasizes visual learning. Parents understand that some children thrive when they can see and visualize information. They support their children's learning style by incorporating visual aids, educational materials, and activities that stimulate their visual senses. These parents provide a visually stimulating environment that enhances their child's curiosity, creativity, and understanding of the world.

Furthermore, parents practicing the Peacock Parenting Style foster self-confidence in their children. They encourage their children to take risks, try new things, and step out of their comfort zone. These parents provide support and guidance, helping their children build resilience and overcome challenges. They celebrate their children's accomplishments and encourage them to believe in their own abilities, promoting a strong sense of self-worth and self-assurance.

By embracing the Peacock Parenting Style, parents can nurture their children's unique individuality, self-expression, and visual learning. Children raised with this style develop a strong sense of self, creativity, and confidence in their abilities. They become comfortable expressing themselves visually and develop a keen eye for detail. They are encouraged to explore their passions and interests, leading to personal growth and a sense of fulfillment.

However, it is important for parents practicing the Peacock Parenting Style to balance their children's visual learning preferences with other learning styles. They should provide a variety of learning experiences to cater to their children's holistic development. By embracing and supporting their children's unique individuality, visual learning style, and self-expression, parents can nurture confident, creative, and thriving children.

Example 1:

Good Peacock Parenting Style (Indian name: Aisha)

Aisha embodies the positive aspects of the Peacock Parenting Style. She celebrates her child's unique individuality and self-expression. Aisha recognizes her child's talents and interests, providing opportunities for personal growth and creative expression. She encourages her child's visual learning style, incorporating visual aids, art, and creative activities into their learning experiences.

Aisha fosters a nurturing environment where her child feels supported and encouraged to explore their passions. She celebrates their achievements, boosting their self-confidence and self-worth. Aisha's parenting style allows her child's true colours to shine, nurturing their creativity, self-expression, and personal development.

Example 2:

Bad Peacock Parenting Style (Indian name: Rajesh)

Rajesh represents a negative example of the Peacock Parenting Style. He fails to celebrate his child's unique individuality and sties their self-expression. Rajesh disregards his child's interests and talents, imposing his own preferences and expectations. He does not provide opportunities for personal growth and creativity, hindering his child's development. Rajesh ignores their visual learning style, failing to support their unique needs and potential. He discourages self-expression and dismisses their creative pursuits. Rajesh's parenting style suppresses his child's self-confidence, creativity, and overall well-being.

These examples highlight the importance of celebrating a child's individuality, fostering self-expression, and embracing their visual learning style. Good Peacock parenting, like Aisha's approach, nurtures a child's unique qualities, provides opportunities for personal growth, and supports their visual learning preferences. In contrast, bad Peacock parenting, as demonstrated by Rajesh, fails to acknowledge a child's individuality, sties their self-expression, and disregards their visual learning needs. By embracing the positive aspects of the Peacock Parenting Style, parents can cultivate an environment where their child's unique qualities are celebrated, their self-expression is encouraged, and their visual learning style is supported, leading to their holistic growth and self-confidence.

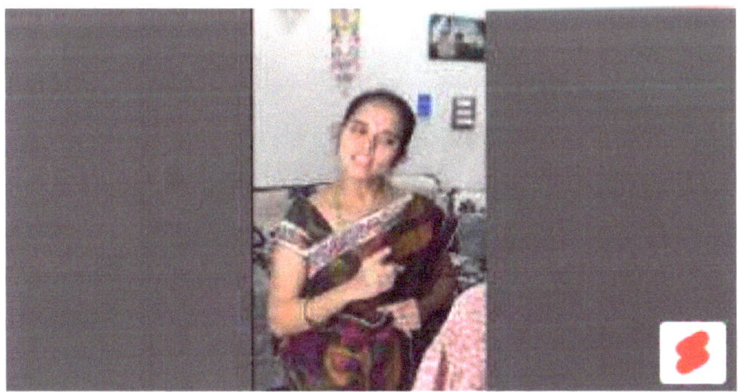

https://www.youtube.com/shorts/OWRkILmaCPs

Chapter 11: The Fox Parenting Style

Parents who adopt the Fox Parenting Style recognize the importance of adaptability in an ever-changing world. They teach their children to be flexible and open-minded, helping them navigate different situations with ease. These parents encourage their children to embrace change as an opportunity for growth and learning, fostering resilience and adaptability.

The Fox Parenting Style emphasizes logical learning and critical thinking. Parents encourage their children to analyse situations, consider different perspectives, and make informed decisions. They provide opportunities for their children to develop problem-solving skills, teaching them to approach challenges with logical reasoning and strategic thinking. These parents foster intellectual curiosity and promote a love for learning, nurturing their children's analytical mindset.

Furthermore, parents practicing the Fox Parenting Style instill a balanced perspective in their children. They teach them to weigh the pros and cons of various options and consider the potential consequences of their choices. These parents emphasize the importance of making well-informed decisions and taking calculated risks. They encourage their children to seek alternatives, explore different solutions, and think critically before acting.

By embracing the Fox Parenting Style, parents can guide their children through life's challenges with resourcefulness and a balanced perspective. Children raised with this style develop adaptability, logical reasoning, and strategic thinking skills. They become adept at problem-solving and decision-making, equipping them with the tools necessary to face obstacles with confidence.

However, it is important for parents practicing the Fox Parenting Style to encourage creativity and emotional intelligence alongside logical learning. They should provide opportunities for their children to explore their artistic side, express their emotions, and develop social skills. By embracing adaptability, logic, and strategic thinking while also nurturing emotional intelligence, parents can cultivate a well-rounded and resilient child who is equipped to thrive in a dynamic world.

Example 1:

Good Fox Parenting Style (Indian name: Rohan)

Rohan embodies the positive aspects of the Fox Parenting Style. He embraces adaptability, logic, and strategic thinking in guiding his child through life's challenges. Rohan encourages his child to be flexible and open-minded, teaching them to embrace change as an opportunity for growth. He fosters their critical thinking skills by engaging them in discussions, encouraging them to analyze situations, and consider different perspectives. Rohan provides opportunities for his child to develop problem-solving abilities, guiding them in making well-informed decisions.

He emphasizes the importance of a balanced perspective, teaching his child to weigh options, consider consequences, and take calculated risks. Rohan's parenting style instills resourcefulness, logical reasoning, and strategic thinking in his child, preparing them to navigate life's complexities with confidence.

Example 2:

Bad Fox Parenting Style (Indian name: Smita)

Smita represents a negative example of the Fox Parenting Style. She fails to embrace adaptability, logic, and strategic thinking in guiding her child.

Smita discourages her child from being open to change, creating a rigid and inflexible environment. She dismisses critical thinking, denying her child the opportunity to develop problem-solving skills. Smita fails to guide her child in making informed decisions and considering consequences, leading to impulsive and hasty choices. She neglects teaching her child a balanced perspective, hindering their ability to weigh options and make sound judgments. Smita's parenting style inhibits resourcefulness, logical reasoning, and strategic thinking in her child, limiting their ability to navigate challenges effectively.

These examples highlight the importance of embracing adaptability, logic, and strategic thinking in the Fox Parenting Style. Good Fox parenting, like Rohan's approach, nurtures a child's adaptability, critical thinking, and problem-solving skills. In contrast, bad Fox parenting, as demonstrated by Smita, fails to foster these important qualities, hindering a child's growth and ability to navigate challenges effectively. By embracing the positive aspects of the Fox Parenting Style, parents can guide their children to become adaptable, logical thinkers who are equipped to approach life's challenges with resourcefulness and a balanced perspective.

https://www.youtube.com/watch?v=nR41mGYK65w

Chapter 12: The Bonobo Parenting Style

Parents who embrace the Bonobo Parenting Style prioritize building strong emotional connections with their children. They create a nurturing and affectionate environment, where love and compassion are at the forefront. These parents prioritize spending quality time with their children, engaging in activities that foster bonding, such as shared hobbies, storytelling, or simply enjoying each other's company. By emphasizing love and affection, they cultivate a sense of security and trust, which forms the foundation for healthy emotional development.

The Bonobo Parenting Style also encourages parents to foster their child's relationships with others. They teach children the value of empathy, kindness, and cooperation. These parents provide opportunities for their children to interact with peers, siblings, and extended family members, allowing them to develop social skills and forge meaningful connections. They teach conflict resolution techniques and encourage their children to communicate effectively, fostering harmonious relationships and emotional intelligence.

Playfulness is a central aspect of the Bonobo Parenting Style. Parents understand the importance of incorporating joy and fun into their child's daily life. They engage in imaginative play, and physical activities, and encourage creativity. Playfulness promotes kinesthetic learning, where children learn through movement, touch, and physical experiences. It enhances their motor skills, cognitive development, and overall well-being.

By adopting the Bonobo Parenting Style, parents can nurture their child's relationships, emotional well-being, and kinesthetic learning. Children raised with this style develop strong emotional intelligence, empathy, and social skills. They experience a sense of belonging and develop a positive outlook on relationships. The emphasis on playfulness fosters their creativity, physical development, and enjoyment of learning.

However, it is important for parents practicing the Bonobo Parenting Style to also provide structure and guidance alongside love and affection. They should set boundaries and provide clear expectations to promote a sense of security and responsibility. By striking a balance between love, compassion, and structure, parents can create a nurturing environment where their children thrive emotionally, socially, and kinesthetically.

Example 1:

Good Bonobo Parenting Style (Indian name: Aisha)

Aisha embodies the positive aspects of the Bonobo Parenting Style. She prioritizes love, affection, and connection in raising her child. Aisha creates a nurturing environment where her child feels safe, loved, and valued. She engages in regular quality time with her child, engaging in activities that foster bonding and emotional connection. Aisha teaches her child the importance of empathy, compassion, and cooperation, encouraging them to develop strong relationships with others. She promotes a playful atmosphere, incorporating fun and joy into their daily life. Aisha understands the value of kinesthetic learning and provides opportunities for her child to learn through movement, exploration, and physical experiences. By embracing the Bonobo Parenting Style, Aisha nurtures her child's emotional well-being, social skills, and kinesthetic learning, creating a foundation for a happy and fulfilling life.

Example 2:

Bad Bonobo Parenting Style (Indian name: Rajesh)

Rajesh represents a negative example of the Bonobo Parenting Style. He fails to prioritize love, affection, and connection in his parenting approach. Rajesh creates an emotionally distant environment where his child lacks a sense of security and warmth.

He neglects to spend quality time with his child, leaving them feeling unloved and disconnected. Rajesh fails to teach his child empathy, compassion, and cooperation, hindering their ability to develop meaningful relationships with others. He disregards the importance of playfulness and kinesthetic learning, resulting in a lack of joy and creativity in his child's life. Rajesh's parenting style inhibits emotional well-being, social development, and kinesthetic learning in his child, impacting their overall growth and happiness.

These examples highlight the importance of adopting the Bonobo Parenting Style in a positive and nurturing manner. Good Bonobo parenting, like Aisha's approach, prioritizes love, affection, connection, and playfulness, fostering emotional well-being, social skills, and kinesthetic learning in the child. In contrast, bad Bonobo parenting, as demonstrated by Rajesh, neglects these crucial aspects, leading to emotional distance, limited social development, and a lack of joy and creativity in the child's life. By embracing the positive aspects of the Bonobo Parenting Style, parents can create a nurturing environment where their children thrive emotionally, socially, and kinesthetically, setting them up for a fulfilling and balanced life.

https://www.youtube.com/shorts/8Eu9Nj_sCH4

Dr. PT Sunderam online profile

YouTube

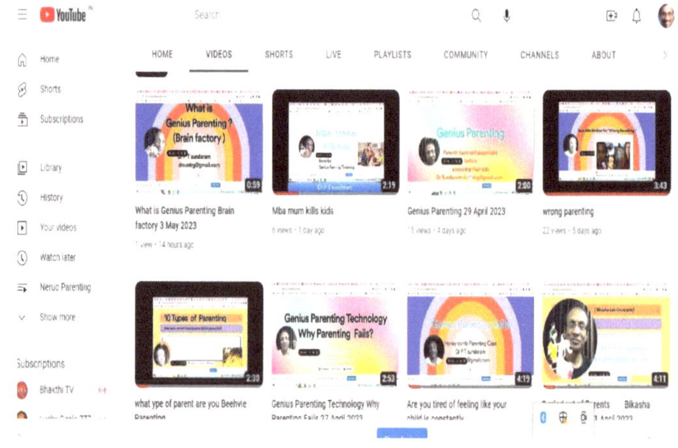

How a Mother can rewire
the Brain Factory
of your kids ?

" I help young parents
to mould
" War kids to Genius kids"
in 4 hours with
Genius Parenting Training "
-Dr.PT Sunderam

Contact
drsuntrg@gmail.com

Instagram

POSTS
REELS
SAVED
TAGGED
MBA -Mother
Kills Kids
Enroll for
Genius Parenting Traiaing
re you a Young Mother with
GENIUS PARENTING
PLAN IN 3 STEPS
Step 1
Step 2
Step 3
Decode your
Brain
Recode your
kids Brain
Encode a
Genius Brain
ven Training model over 10 years
with 10,000 Young Parents
GPP Tool kit
Genius Parenting Plan

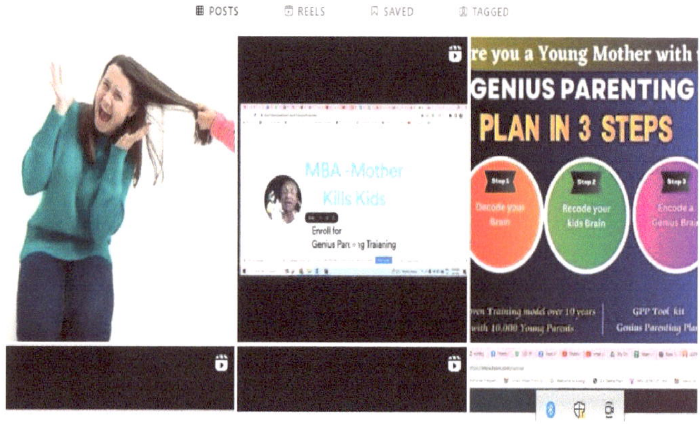

Facebook

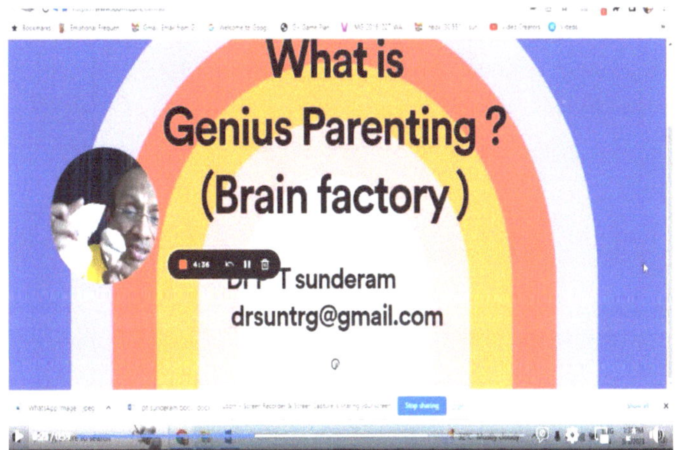
What is
Genius Parenting ?
(Brain factory)
Dr P T sunderam
drsuntrg@gmail.com

BOOK HERE

FREE CONSULTANCY COUPONS

Kindly fill in the form with the eligibility criteria and
enclose screenshot evidence to email

"drsuntrg@gmail.com"

Client Intake Form

Mother Name: _______________________

Age of the mother: _________________________

City : ____________________________

Phone Number: _________________________

Email: ____________________________

Eligibility Criteria

(within the first 10 day of purchase of the book)

1. I have read the book _____________________ (mention the title of the book)

2. I am impressed with _____________________ (chapter of the book)

3. I am including the screenshot of the lines for clarification (screenshot)

4. I am including the photo of me and my kid

5. I want consultation for the following three points

(i) _____ ____

____

(ii) ____

____

(iii) ____

____

Re Parenting Tools
Make ur kids Listen to you
zoo parenting system
Dr P T sunderam
Asia Top 1% Parenting 3.0 coach,
years journey with 25,000 Joyful PARENTS
Parenting secrets
A must skill for every Super MOM
With Baghban Template Work Book
REVERSE
BROKEN RELATIONSHIP
IN 3 DAYS
WITHOUT COUNSELLING
PTS MIND CLUB
A 2 STEP JOURNEY TO REJOIN YOUR PARTNER TODAY
India First Married Couples Thought Re programing Relationship Expert Mentor
Dr P T Sunderam M S
21 TRUE STORIES
The Invisible Wounds of Dysfunctional Relationship
Counselling and NLP can Reinvent Your Life
P.T.Sunderam PhD
Dr. P. T. Sunderam
INDIAS 1 ST MARRIED COUPLES MENTOR
7 Templates to save your Marriage"
without counselling before it is
"Damaged"
Transformed 25,000 youth in last 25 years with this templates"
work book for "Marriage Rescue Plan in 3 steps" work shop
TRUE STORY
HOW COUPLES CAME OUT
OF DYSFUNCTIONAL RELATIONSHIPS
USING NLP TECHNIQUES
PT SUNDERAM PH D
25 years
Practical
with 25,000 +
COUPLES
4 Daignostic NLP Re Parentig tool
for every Married Couples
website: www.ptsunderam.com
e-mail id: drsuntrg@gmail